WITHDRAWN

Presented to

Kingwood Branch Library

By

**Friends of the
Kingwood Library**

Harris County
Public Library
your pathway to knowledge

CRIME AND DETECTION

FAMOUS PRISONS

Crime and Detection series

- Criminal Terminology
- Cyber Crime
- Daily Prison Life
- Death Row and Capital Punishment
- Domestic Crime
- Famous Prisons
- Famous Trials
- Forensic Science
- Government Intelligence Agencies
- Hate Crimes
- The History and Methods of Torture
- The History of Punishment
- International Terrorism
- Major Unsolved Crimes
- Organized Crime
- Protecting Yourself Against Criminals
- Race and Crime
- Serial Murders
- The United States Justice System
- The War Against Drugs

CRIME AND DETECTION

FAMOUS PRISONS

JOAN LOCK

MASON CREST PUBLISHERS
www.masoncrest.com

Mason Crest Publishers, Inc.
370 Reed Road
Broomall, PA 19008
(866) MCP-BOOK (toll free)
www.masoncrest.com

13 12 11 10 09 08 07 06 05   10 9 8 7 6 5 4 3 2

Library of Congress Cataloging-in-Publication Data

Lock, Joan.
   Famous prisons / Joan Lock.
      v. cm. — (Crime and detection)
Includes bibliographical references and index.
Contents: Alcatraz Federal Penitentiary, California — Up river: Sing Sing Prison, New York
State — Halfway to Hell: Dartmoor Prison — The big house: San Quentin State Penitentiary,
California — Ireland's model
prison: Mountjoy, Dublin — Going around in circles: Stateville Penitentiary, Joliet, Illinois.
   ISBN 1-59084-380-0
   1. Prisons—Juvenile literature. [1. Prisons.] I. Title. II. Series.
   HV8705.F36 2003
   365—dc21

                              2003000477

Editorial and design by
Amber Books Ltd.
Bradley's Close
47–77 White Lion Street
London N1 9PF
www.amberbooks.co.uk

Project Editor: Michael Spilling
Design: Floyd Sayers
Picture Research: Natasha Jones

Printed and bound in Malaysia

CONTENTS

Introduction

From the moment in the Book of Genesis when Cain's envy of his brother Abel erupted into violence, crime has been an inescapable feature of human life. Every society ever known has had its own sense of how things ought to be, its deeply held views on how men and women should behave. Yet in every age there have been individuals ready to break these rules for their own advantage: they must be resisted if the community is to thrive.

This exciting and vividly illustrated new series sets out the history of crime and detection from the earliest times to the present day, from the empires of the ancient world to the towns and cities of the 21st century. From the commandments of the great religions to the theories of modern psychologists, it considers changing attitudes toward offenders and their actions. Contemporary crime is examined in its many different forms: everything from racial hatred to industrial espionage, from serial murder to drug trafficking, from international terrorism to domestic violence.

The series looks, too, at the work of those men and women entrusted with the task of overseeing and maintaining the law, from judges and court officials to police officers and other law enforcement agents. The tools and techniques at their disposal are described and vividly illustrated, and the ethical issues they face concisely and clearly explained.

All in all, the *Crime and Detection* series provides a comprehensive and accessible account of crime and detection, in theory and in practice, past and present.

CHARLIE FULLER
Executive Director, International Association of Undercover Officers

Left: A cell from Alcatraz Prison, the notorious California high-security penitentiary perched on a small island in San Francisco Bay. Despite its fame, Alcatraz was a small prison that was used for just 30 years and housed no more than 250 prisoners at any one time.

Alcatraz Federal Penitentiary, California

"Alcatraz" is the Spanish word for "pelican." It was early explorers who gave the island this name because it had once been a bird habitat. The first buildings on the island were a lighthouse and a fortress. The fortress was built in reaction to the influx of sailing ships during the Gold Rush of 1848–1849.

The most surprising thing about Alcatraz Federal Penitentiary, perching dramatically on a rock in San Francisco Bay, is how few prisoners actually stayed there and how short a time it was in operation. Throughout its history, the prison never held more than 250 inmates at one time and was open for business for less than 30 years (1934–1963). However, its fame is largely due to the type of prisoners it held—the very worst—and by the way that Alcatraz was dramatized by Hollywood, capturing the imagination of millions of people.

THE PRISONERS

Down the years, the island housed military prisoners of various kinds: Civil War combatants, enemy aliens and spies during World War I, and finally, U.S. soldiers in need of extra discipline. Then later, in the 1930s, when the United States found it had a gangster problem, Alcatraz was used to put many of the mobsters behind bars.

Left: This photograph shows a corridor in the main Alcatraz cell block. These long walkways were known to the prisoners as Broadway, Seedy Street, and Michigan Avenue, and were overlooked at each end by a gun gallery.

This is how Alcatraz looks from the air. The large, white, central building is the cell house. On the edges of the island are the staff housing, docks, power plant, factory, and other support buildings.

Violent and disruptive prisoners cause security problems in jails. Thus, it seemed like a good idea to lump the worst of them together into a single, secure place. In 1933, the War Department relinquished Alcatraz Island, which was acquired by the Justice Department. By 1934, it had been refitted and opened as a maximum-security federal penitentiary.

The prisoners came from all over the United States: mail-train bandit Roy Gardner; bank robber and kidnapper "Machine Gun" Kelly; Alvin Karpis, who had been named Public Rat Number One by J. Edgar Hoover; and his fellow kidnapper, Dock Barker—a remnant of the infamous Barker family. (Ma Barker and son Fred were killed in a shoot-out with the police. Herman committed suicide when trapped during a bank robbery, and Lloyd was doing time in Leavenworth Prison.)

The Rock—as Alcatraz was also known—was home to the highest

profile gangster of them all, the murderous Al Capone, who was responsible for the 1929 St. Valentine's Day Massacre of his rivals. Capone was brought down in 1931, not by the Feds, but by the Internal Revenue Service, for tax evasion and other offenses.

Alphonse (Al) Capone, born in Brooklyn, New York, in 1899. Achieving worldwide notoriety as a racketeer during the Prohibition period in Chicago, he was sent to Alcatraz after a conviction for tax evasion.

DAILY LIFE ON ALCATRAZ

The prison was built to house 450 prisoners. However, the fact that there were never more than 250 prisoners on the island at one time helped authorities to stick to the rule, "one prisoner, one cell"—important for the maintenance of discipline. The windowless cells were 10 feet by 4 feet, 6 inches (3 by 1.5 m). They were stacked in three tiers and overlooked at each end by gun galleries patrolled by armed guards. The cells were strategically placed upon a hill in the center of the island.

Alcatraz was a minimum-privilege prison, which at first operated a silent system. Prisoners were not allowed newspapers or radios, and could speak only when absolutely necessary. At times, as many as one-quarter of the inmates were not even allowed to leave their cells to go out to work, but were on permanent lockup. When extra discipline was needed, there was the dreadful old dungeon or punishment cells on D Block.

Inevitably, inmates made accusations of brutality against the guards. Clark Howard, who wrote the book *Six Against the Rock*, claimed some guards could be unfeeling, or even sadistic. However, others, like the "Candy Bar Kid," who most days chucked a chocolate bar into one or another of the cells, did their best to make the prisoners' lives more bearable.

Alcatraz had always been an expensive prison to run. All supplies had to be shipped there and the waste taken away. Transporting dangerous men under guard from all over the United States was also costly, and the elderly prison buildings were in dire need of renovation. As a result, in 1963, "deactivation" began. Shortly afterward, a group of Sioux Native Americans claimed the island, citing an 1868 treaty that allowed them the right to any unoccupied government land. Today, Alcatraz is a favorite tourist attraction operated by the National Park Services.

"MACHINE GUN" KELLY GOES TO ALCATRAZ

During the 1920s and early 1930s, the kidnapping of wealthy men by mobsters had become such a problem that the FBI established a direct

ISLAND PRISONS

Alcatraz is not the only well-known island prison. Devil's Island, the French penal settlement off the coast of South America, was first opened in 1852 to accommodate prisoners suffering from leprosy. It became notorious for its harsh conditions. Later, the prison was used mostly for political prisoners, including the famous Alfred Dreyfus (pictured), the subject of numerous books and movies.

The most famous island prisoner of all was Napoleon Bonaparte, who, after escaping from exile on the Isle of Elba, was defeated at the Battle of Waterloo in 1815. To make sure he stayed captive, he was sent this time to the tiny island of St. Helena, which is out in the middle of the Atlantic Ocean halfway between Africa and South America. He died there in 1821.

The United States has other offshore prisons, such as Ryker's Island in Bowerie Bay, New York, and McNeil Island in Puget Sound, Washington State. None have achieved the notoriety of Alcatraz, possibly because they did not have Hollywood on their doorsteps and did not house only the most dangerous and deadliest of public enemies.

George "Machine Gun" Kelly outside his cell. Along with many other gangsters, he sought to make money from kidnapping; unluckily for him, his victim, Charles F. Urschel, proved to be too observant, leading to Kelly's identification and eventual arrest.

"kidnapping line" to the office of J. Edgar Hoover. The wife of Charles F. Urschel, a millionaire in the oil business of Oklahoma City, used the line on Saturday, July 22, 1933. She reported that she and her husband were playing bridge after dinner with another couple on their porch when two men appeared. One of them was brandishing a submachine gun. The intruders kidnapped both men, but let the friend go when they ascertained he was not Urschel. A $200,000 ransom was demanded and paid, and Urschel was duly released.

However, the kidnappers had made an unfortunate choice of victim. Although blindfolded, Charles F. Urschel proved an observant victim. For example, when he had heard a plane overhead, he asked his kidnappers what time it was. He also noticed the noises of cows and guinea fowls outside the house where he was imprisoned and the creaking of a nearby windlass. He also made a mental note of the strong mineral taste of the water he was given.

The plane turned out to be the daily flight from Fort Worth to Amarillo (both in Texas) and back. The Feds worked out that, at the times noted (9:45 A.M. and 5:45 P.M.), it would be over the small town of Paradise. Agents visited nearby farms and homesteads, posing as bankers offering loans, and found one that kept cows and guinea fowls and had a creaking windlass. Mopping their brows and claiming to be fatigued, they requested glasses of water. It had a strong mineral taste.

It transpired that the farmer's stepdaughter was the wife of bootlegger and bank robber "Machine Gun" Kelly, who liked to boast that he could write his name on the side of a barn door with bullets. Kelly was tried, convicted, and duly sent to Alcatraz.

At Alcatraz, Kelly refused to become involved in escape attempts on the grounds that, since he was not a murderer, he would some day be released. He died of a heart attack in 1954 while still in prison. His wife, Katherine, who was reputed to have urged him to kill Urschel, was released from prison in 1958.

AL CAPONE ON ALCATRAZ

Al Capone did not prove popular with Alcatraz inmates. Not only had too many of their pals been killed by his henchmen, but also some lifers resented his easy 10-year stint for tax dodging and his obvious wealth. The **warden** declined his offers to pay for a bigger exercise yard and to provide new instruments for the band, in which he played a bejeweled banjo that his wife bought for him. Whenever he was told stories about hardships back home, he directed his wife to distribute money to the relatives of inmates. When the warden told him to stop this, Capone had to deny their requests, which caused more resentment, as did his refusal to become involved in escape attempts. And there were several of those.

Al Capone left the island in 1939 to spend a final year in a new prison on Terminal Island in Los Angeles Harbor. Due to attempts on his life, he was afraid to go out into the yard during Sunday afternoon recreation time, and even became frightened to come out of his cell. He was taken off laundry work and put on solo jobs inside. The pressure (and the disease syphilis) got to him, and Capone's mind began to go. Indeed, he spent the last couple of years on the island in the prison hospital.

ESCAPE ATTEMPTS

In May 1938, three bank robbers, Whitey Franklin, Jimmy Lucas, and Sandy Limerick, jumped an unarmed guard in the Alcatraz furniture workshop. They beat him to death with a claw hammer and made their way up to the roof. Here, they rushed toward one of the armed lookout towers, throwing hammers and wrenches through the windows from all sides.

Tower guard Hal Stites, an easygoing man and one of the Rock's most popular officers, did not panic. He drew his .45 handgun and fired at Limerick, hitting him in the head and killing him instantly. Then, he turned and fired at the other two. Franklin went down, hit in the shoulder. Finding his handgun empty, Stites grabbed the rifle and pointed it at Lucas, who put his hands up. However, Franklin had recovered and was lunging

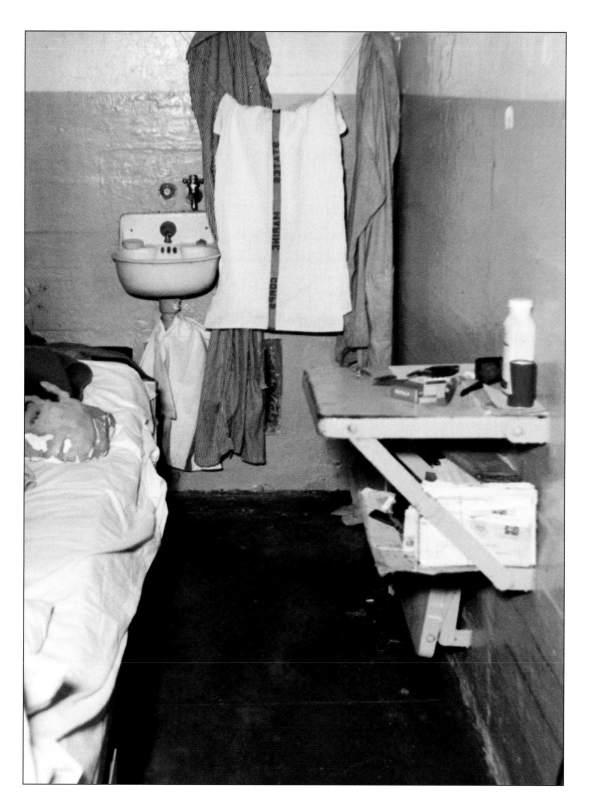

This is one of the Alcatraz cells from which three prisoners escaped in 1962. On the bed is the dummy head used to hide the fact that the inmate was missing. Simple deceptions such as this could buy the escapees extra time.

forward again. Stites swung around and got him in the other shoulder. The escape attempt was over.

THE BIG BLAST-OUT

In 1939, Dock Barker was shot dead when he and four other prisoners made an escape attempt. Seven years later, around midday on May 2, 1946, the Big Blast-Out began. Hal Stites would not be so lucky this time. Three convicts were watching Bert Burch, the guard on the west gun gallery, waiting for him to go through the door into D Block where "Crazy" Sam Shockley just happened to be going berserk in his cell.

The east gun gallery was unmanned. During the 15 minutes Burch stayed out of sight, Officer Bill Miller was attacked and knocked unconscious by bank robber Bernie Coy and kidnapper (of a policeman) Marvin Hubbard. They dragged Miller to Cell 403, took the keys, and released the surly and vicious Dutch Cretzer and 19-year-old Native American, "The Indio Kid," both murderers.

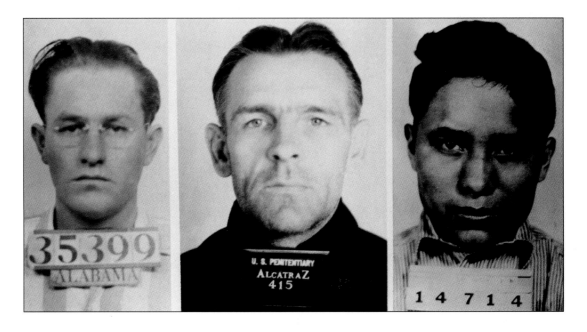

Three ringleaders of what became known as the "Battle of Alcatraz." From left to right, Marvin Hubbard, Bernard Paul Coy, and "The Indio Kid," who was the only one to survive the vicious and deadly struggle.

Bernie Coy, who was lean and fit, managed to climb to the gun gallery, to which he gained access with bar spreaders stolen from the plumbing shop. When Bert Burch came back through the door from D Block, he was attacked. He fought back, but was bludgeoned with his own rifle butt. Coy passed down the guard's keys, automatic pistol, and the Springfield rifle to the other escapees below. Now armed, they broke into upper D Block, where they released 12 prisoners, who ran out and down the stairs shouting, "The cons have taken over, let's go." However, only two of them left the block: "Crazy" Sam Shockley and Buddy Thompson, who had killed a Texan cop in cold blood.

Soon, four more guards were captured and dragged to Cell 403. The prisoners' plan was to storm out, keeping the guards as hostages, and then boarding the prison **launch**, which was arriving at the dock. However, the escapees were unable to find the vital key 107, which would let them out of the block. Bill Miller denied all knowledge of it. Desperately, the convicts tried all the other keys in case one was deliberately mislabeled, but to no effect. Eventually, they found the real key hidden in Cell 403's toilet bowl. However, one of the keys they had tried had jammed in the lock. When they finally pried it out, the real key would not work—the lock jammed automatically when forced.

THE BATTLE OF ALCATRAZ

Unanswered phones indicated that something was amiss in the cell house, so Guard Captain Henry Weinhold went in. He, too, was captured, as were three more officers who tried to find him. The prisoners' plans now changed. They would have to bargain their way out with the hostages, but they needed to take out the tower guards to stop them from firing.

Coy managed to wound one of them with the rifle, but the shots finally alerted the whole prison and the siren was sounded. Armed guards were sent into the west gun gallery, but four of these were brought down, wounded by Coy. Then Dutch Cretzer joined in with the handgun and

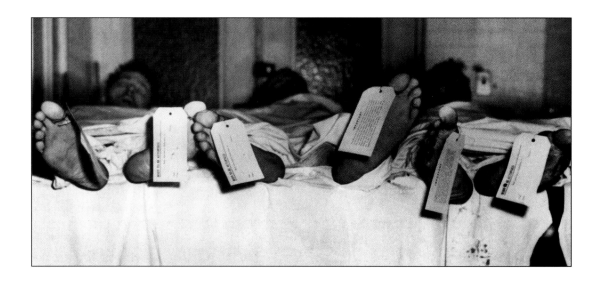

The tagged toes of the bodies of three of the prisoners who died in the Battle of Alcatraz. From left to right, Dutch Cretzer, Bernie Coy, and Marvin Hubbard. Many attempted escapes and break- outs ended in the deaths of both prisoners and prison guards.

shot Hal Stites in the stomach. Stites died shortly afterward. Any hope of a deal was off.

Cretzer beat Miller mercilessly, kicking him and stamping on his head, because, by hiding key 107, he had foiled the escape. Thompson kept insisting that Cretzer should kill all the **screws** now in Cell 402 and 403 so that there would be no one to testify against them. Shockley egged him on. Cretzer did his best: first, he shot Captain Henry Weinhold point-blank in the chest, Cecil Corwin in the face, and the unconscious Bill Miller in the body. Then he reloaded and moved on to empty the .45 automatic into Cell 402. Lt. Joe Simpson was hit in the stomach and chest, and Robert Baker in the arm and leg. The other guards played dead. Eventually, colleagues managed to get in to release their fellow officers, although another officer was shot in the process.

Late that afternoon, a squad of U.S. Marines landed on the island and crowds began lining the mainland shore to watch. The battle continued until 9:20 A.M. on the third day. By then, the block had been bombarded by bazookas, mortar shells, and grenades, and sprayed with machine gun fire. Cretzer, Hubbard, and Coy were dead, as was Officer Bill Miller.

Thompson, Shockley, and the Indio Kid were later tried for the murder of the two guards. The other officers survived, although for some it had been touch and go. The Indio Kid was sent back to the Rock, now with two life sentences plus 99 years. Shockley and Thompson went to the gas chamber at San Quentin.

THE BIRDMAN OF ALCATRAZ

Robert Stroud did not arrive at Alcatraz until 1942. According to a senior guard, Captain Philip Bergen, Stroud was not the placid, gentlemanly scientist portrayed by Burt Lancaster in the movie *Birdman of Alcatraz*. "He was a Jekyll and Hyde character, and you never knew when he got up in the morning which one he would be."

In fact, Stroud was already in prison for murder, having beaten a fellow prisoner nearly to death while at McNeil Island Penitentiary and murdering a guard at Leavenworth Prison.

Surprisingly, the so-called "Birdman of Alcatraz" never kept birds on the island despite the fact that it had once been a bird habitat. It was at Leavenworth Federal Penitentiary that he had turned his cell into an aviary. He was not able to do this at Alcatraz, but continued to write about birds while imprisoned there.

Up River—Sing Sing Prison, New York State

Being sent upriver, the expression for receiving a prison sentence, originated with the establishment of Sing Sing State Penitentiary on the banks of the Hudson River 25 miles (40 km) from New York City.

The prison, built by convicts, is famous for its electric chair. In 1825, New York State had two prisons. Newgate, named after London's most famous lockup (jail), was built in Greenwich Village in 1797. Overcrowding there led to the construction of Auburn State Penitentiary between 1816 and 1825. However, Auburn, which is just south of Lake Ontario, proved neither near enough to New York City nor large enough to house the many criminals bred in America's most populous city. Consequently, in 1825, the strongest of Auburn's prisoners were chosen for the task of leveling a site at Sing Sing (named after Sin Sinck Native Americans) and building the prison that was to hold them.

Once Sing Sing was built, the authorities decided that the inmates could work at nearby quarries and, in fact, their backbreaking labor was to provide the stone for Grace Church on Broadway, New York University, and City Hall in Albany.

Left: Sing Sing will always be associated with execution by the electric chair. Over 600 prisoners were executed there before 1963, as were several movie characters, including a gangster played by James Cagney in *Angels with Dirty Faces* (1938).

This photograph shows the interior of one of the Auburn-style cell blocks at Sing Sing in the late 19th century. Many young offenders, including those in their late teens, were among the inmates confined there under maximum security.

ATTEMPTING REFORM IN THE "HOUSE OF FEAR"

Elam Lynds, the first warden of Sing Sing, ruled using cruelty, semistarvation, and the lash (whip). It was his reputation that earned the prison the name "House of Fear." A respite for the prisoners came with the appointment in 1840 of Warden D.L. Seymour, who put controls on the ferocious whippings and introduced privileges, such as allowing prisoners to receive letters. However, the prison was less profitable under his control, and he was accused of coddling the prisoners. So Lynds was brought back.

However, Prison Inspector John Worth Edmonds, who had been instrumental in the reappointment of Lynds, at last realized what was happening. He also observed that conditions for female prisoners were often worse than that of the men. Women were subjected to degrading treatment and put under the supervision of male guards. So he re-established some of the privileges and in 1844, appointed Eliza Farnham to run the women's wing. Eliza Farnham was a disciple of English prison reformer Elizabeth Fry, who advocated separate prisons for women, administered by women, and the provision of religious training and rehabilitation. The new matron ended the rule of silence, introduced an educational program, installed a piano, placed potted plants on the windowsills, and gave out candy on holidays.

Her reforms were met with fierce resistance from the warden. Unfortunately, the fact that she was interested in **phrenology** made her vulnerable because it was thought by some to be downright kooky and by others to relieve criminals of responsibility for their crimes. Forced to restore the rule of silence and discontinue her other reforms, Farnham resigned in 1848. The women's wing was closed in 1877, and women prisoners were farmed out to various local jails.

OLD SPARKY

The electric chair was first introduced at Auburn in 1890 on the grounds that the new electricity would provide a more humane method of execution than hanging or the firing squads that some states used. The question of whether electrocution is indeed a humane method or (as some claim) a painful one has never been settled. The only people who really know are not available for comment.

Fifteen states acquired electric chairs, but the method was never adopted outside the United States. The first to die by "Old Sparky," or the "Thunderbolt," at Sing Sing was Harris A. Smiler in 1891. Between then and 1963, when the chair was decommissioned, 614 men and women were electrocuted at the prison. An infamous couple who died in the electric chair was Ruth Snyder, dubbed by the press "The Granite Woman," and her lover, Henry Judd Gray. Ruth, aged 32, had already tried to kill her dull, 45-year-old husband Albert several times before she met Gray. In an effort to cash in on Albert's $96,000 life insurance policy, she had tried gassing him, poisoning him, and suffocating him.

On March 20, 1927, Ruth roped in Gray, a 35-year-old corset salesman, for another attempt on her husband's life. When Albert was asleep, the worse for drink, they murdered him with the aid of chloroform, picture wire, and a window-sash weight, and then staged a break-in, which left Ruth tied up and gagged.

However, police found inconsistencies in her story and Gray's name in her diary. They tricked Ruth into believing that her lover had confessed. She admitted to the murder, but swore she had not struck a single blow.

When they went to the electric chair at Sing Sing on January 12, 1928, a press photographer with a camera strapped to his ankle managed to get the now-famous blurred photograph of Ruth's death **throes**.

A HUMANE BUT FIRM POLICY

Conditions at Sing Sing improved further at the turn of the century. The humiliating **lockstep**, which forced prisoners to shuffle along together with chains around their ankles, went in 1900, and the black-and-white striped uniform was abolished in 1904. In 1913, Warden Clancy began to allow

This haunting picture shows the electrocution of murderess Ruth Snyder at Sing Sing in 1928. Another infamous couple to die there 25 years later were the Communist spies Ethel and Julius Rosenberg, accused of passing atomic secrets to the Soviet Union.

prisoners out of their cells on Sunday mornings, and later, this was extended to Saturday afternoon and all day Sunday. Previously, they had spent the whole weekend locked up. In 1914, the rule of silence was lifted. A new warden, Thomas Mott Osborne, tried to loosen things up even further, but he, too, was accused of coddling prisoners and allowing indiscipline. He resigned under pressure.

Sing Sing Warden Lewis E. Lawes. His book, *Twenty Thousand Years in Sing Sing* (1932), was used as the basis of a 1933 movie starring Spencer Tracy.

AUBURN AND PENNSYLVANIA SYSTEMS

During the 19th century, two prison systems evolved in the United States: the Auburn and the Pennsylvania. Both enforced the rule of silence, but the Pennsylvania, or silent and separate system, kept prisoners in permanent solitary confinement. They ate, worked, and slept in their cells, which were slightly larger than normal. On the rare occasions they were allowed out, they had to wear masks. The idea was to prevent cross-contamination so that they did not leave prison with more vices than when they had arrived. Also, prison discipline was easier to maintain when the prisoners were not allowed to mix.

The writer Charles Dickens was horrified by the Pennsylvania system he saw at Eastern State Penitentiary. He thought it must be like being buried alive. Nonetheless, Pentonville "Model Prison" in London, England, was built and operated on the Pennsylvania lines.

Under the Auburn system, inmates were taken out of their cells during the day to work alongside each other in quarries and factories and were confined to their cells only in the evenings and at night. Discipline was harder to enforce in Auburn-run prisons, which resulted in the liberal use of punishments, the wearing of easily identifiable striped uniforms, and marching (or shuffling) in lockstep.

Finally, the prisoners of Sing Sing got lucky in 1920 with the appointment of Lewis E. Lawes, who had studied the writings of criminologists. Lawes read the works of Cesare Beccaria, who advocated the prevention of crime by education, and Cesare Lombroso, who believed there was a recognizable criminal type. He read August Drahms, who claimed that criminals had special physical characteristics, such as narrower foreheads, crooked noses, larger ears, and longer arms. He read about the work of the prison reformers Elizabeth Fry and Benjamin Rush, a signatory of the Declaration of Independence, who was active in prison reform in Pennsylvania in the late 18th century. There was also the work of the Englishman John Howard, who began his crusade after experiencing dreadful prison conditions while he was held captive by the French in 1755. Today, organizations bearing Howard's name still exist in both Britain and the United States.

Lawes came to the conclusion that a humane but firm policy would be the most effective, and was able to generate support for this. He oversaw a huge rebuilding program, which included a chapel, hospital, mess hall, barbershop, library, a gymnasium, and classrooms for 1,100 inmates. A former New York City newspaper editor convicted of murder was allowed both to edit the prison newspaper and erect a large birdhouse in the dreary grounds, which were also beautified with shrubs and flowerbeds.

LIFE IN SING SING

Like Alcatraz, Sing Sing was a backdrop for several movies. The most memorable was *Angels with Dirty Faces* (1938), in which a gangster played by James Cagney goes screaming to the electric chair so as to discourage slum boys from a life of crime. The most prominent of the real-life gangsters at Sing Sing during the 1930s was Sicilian godfather Lucky Luciano. As well as drug peddling, extortion, and brothel running, Lucky was one of four men who organized the hit squad Murder, Inc., said to have been responsible for over 400 killings.

He earned his nickname due to his ability to avoid arrest, but, like Capone, was finally brought down (in 1936) for one of his lesser offenses. Three women gave evidence that he had forced them into prostitution. Upon his release in 1946, he was deported as an undesirable alien.

Today, Sing Sing houses around 2,400 prisoners, mostly in maximum-

Thomas Mott Osborn (right), Sing Sing Warden (1914–16), standing in a cell block with two guards. He resigned under pressure after being accused of destroying prison discipline with his reforms. The regime at Sing Sing was finally relaxed under Warden Lewis E. Lawes.

James Cagney (pictured) played a notorious hoodlum in the movie *Angels with Dirty Faces*. Here, he is shown in a typically aggressive pose.

Here, an inmate talks to the Captain of the Guard just before his release in 1940. Prisoners had more day-to-day contact with these officers than with the warden.

security conditions. More than half are African-American, and one-third are Hispanic. The guards, too, are mostly from the ethnic minorities. Like many such prisons, it remains a violent place with frequent attacks on fellow prisoners and their guards. Some attacks are fatal.

Corrections Officer David Luther recalled the first time he doubted his choice of profession. An inmate had thrown cups of feces, urine, and caustic soap over him. "I was covered from head to foot," he told *AFSCME Public Employee Magazine* (July/August 1998). "That smell. The skin on my face was burning. My eyes were burning. I couldn't see." He showered three times and was taken to a hospital, but his treatment was hampered by the fact that the prisoner exercised his right to keep his medical records secret so that David could not discover which diseases he might have been

COLD WAR SPIES

Julius and Ethel Rosenberg were American Communists revealed as part of a transatlantic spy ring uncovered by the capture of Klaus Fuchs. German-born Fuchs was a naturalized Briton who passed atomic secrets to the Soviets. The Rosenbergs and Ethel's brother, David Greenglass, were employed at Los Alamos Nuclear Research Station. They were also accused of passing atomic secrets to the Soviet Union.

The evidence against the Rosenbergs came largely from David Greenglass, who, to save his own skin, had become a prosecution witness. The defense argued that the death penalty applied for spying during wartime only and when the Rosenbergs had divulged secrets during World War II, the Soviet Union had been an ally of the U.S. Despite numerous appeals for clemency from many Western countries and inside the U.S., the Rosenbergs were sent to the electric chair at Sing Sing on June 19, 1953.

Heavily guarded while on a train heading for Sing Sing and the electric chair in 1941 are gangsters Louis Capone (left, no relation of Al) and Mendy Weiss, who were convicted of murdering Joseph Rosen. Capone and Weiss were both members of the brutal gang known as "Murder, Inc.," which was the enforcement arm of the infamous National Crime Syndicate run out of New York by gangster boss Albert Anastasia and labor racketeer Louis "Lepke" Buchalter.

exposed to—and some inmates have AIDS and hepatitis. Undeterred, Luther quotes Nathaniel Hawthorne's story of a man who searched for 20 years to find the unforgivable sin. His heart became hardened, "and that was the unforgivable sin."

Halfway to Hell— Dartmoor Prison

Like Alcatraz, Dartmoor Prison, in Devon, England, is situated on an island. However, it is an island surrounded not by sea, but by endless miles of bleak and desolate moorland. This wild land is known as Dartmoor, southern England's largest expanse of wilderness. The only living creatures to be seen on the 365 square miles (945 sq km) of moorland are wild ponies and the occasional flock of sheep. When the mist, rain, and freezing fog come down over the miles and miles of rough terrain and granite outcrops, escapees can become hopelessly lost and dreadfully cold and hungry. Arthur Conan Doyle found Dartmoor to be the perfect setting for his ghostly Sherlock Holmes mystery novel, **The Hound of the Baskervilles.**

THE EARLY DAYS OF DARTMOOR

Surprisingly, soon after its opening, the prison was to house several thousand Americans. It had originally been built to accommodate the French prisoners who were overcrowding prison **hulks** in Plymouth Harbour. They had been captured during the Napoleonic wars, but by 1809, began slinging their hammocks from the iron posts in Dartmoor's freezing dormitories. The five buildings were designed to hold 1,000 men each. Yet here, too, overcrowding quickly became so bad that volunteer inmates were paid to build additional prison blocks. However, numbers still increased until there were nearly 10,000 prisoners.

Left: An interior view of the modern Dartmoor Prison. Inmates of the old buildings included U.S. prisoners of war (1813) and Eamon de Valera (1916), who was to become Ireland's first prime minister.

The sanitation was primitive, dormitories were damp and cold, and prison rations, although primarily of good quality, were short on quantity. Unsurprisingly, disease soon became rife. In the first year, more than 460 prisoners died during a measles outbreak. Smallpox, typhus, and pneumonia also took their toll. Such diseases were common outside the prison, but the overcrowding inside caused them to spread sometimes to epidemic proportions.

In 1813, American prisoners from the War of 1812 began to arrive. With them came many British prisoners who had "refused to fight against their own" (the Americans). While some prisoners existed like primitives, not washing and also gambling away their clothes, some of the wealthier Frenchmen ("Les Lords") lived in style, even employing other prisoners as servants and cooks.

The inmates themselves largely organized discipline within the prison. The Americans elected their own committees and even sent criers throughout the prison to announce their suggestions, to which each man would answer "aye" or "nay." Every day, an open market was held within the prison walls and farmers and traders came to sell their goods, such as tobacco, coffee, poultry, and produce. Those who were employed in the prison or who worked as builders had wages to spend. Others began counterfeiting British currency (the Americans were best at this) or carving beautiful objects from bone and wood to use as barter. Today, some of these ornaments, snuffboxes, and model ships can be seen in museums and antique shops, where they fetch high prices.

Gambling became rife, and brawls, riots, duels, suicides, and murders quite common. However, as time went on, a school of music, dancing classes, a glee club, a theater, and a boxing academy were also set up.

A NEW ROLE FOR DARTMOOR

When the wars with France ended in 1814–1815, the French prisoners were released. By December 1814, the hostilities with the United States had also ceased. However, long delays in **repatriation** caused tensions to rise. In April 1815, there was a pitched battle between the (now technically free) prisoners and the militia, which resulted in the deaths of nine Americans. This became known as the Princetown Massacre.

In 1868, the prison governor had two memorial **obelisks** erected to the memory of the French and the 268 Americans who died at Dartmoor, and in 1928, the American Daughters of 1812 added a memorial gateway to the U.S. cemetery. Bad as conditions were, however, they were superior to those of most of the prisoner of war camps in which many thousands from both sides died during the American Civil War.

A solitary walker moves across the bleak landscape of Dartmoor at dusk. Escaping prisoners quickly became lost there, and the moor's bleakness inspired Arthur Conan Doyle to use it as the setting for *The Hound of the Baskervilles.*

ANDREW J. GARVEY.—PHOTOGRAPHED BY GURNEY & SONS.—[SEE PAGE 281.]

THE TICHBORNE CASE—THE CLAIMANT.

THE TICHBORNE CASE.

THE announcement of the jury in the celebrated TICHBORNE case that they had heard sufficient evidence on which to base a verdict brought to an unexpectedly abrupt termination one of the most remarkable trials on record. It had lasted 114 days. The most eminent counsel in the kingdom were engaged on both sides, and no trial, perhaps, ever excited more interest in Europe and America. Though the case has gone against the claimant, there are, no doubt, many persons who still consider him the lawful heir to the TICHBORNE baronetcy. If he be an impostor, as the jury have decided, his attempt was certainly one of the most remarkable conspiracies to obtain possession of a title and a large estate of which we have any record in modern times.

The story, in brief outline, is this: In 1853 ROGER TICHBORNE, eldest son of Sir JAMES TICHBORNE, left home for a long absence. He sailed from Havre on the 1st of March for Valparaiso, at which port he arrived in June, the same year. During his stay in South America, which lasted from this time until the 20th of April in the following year, he traveled extensively, from Rio to Buenos Ayres, crossing the Cordilleras, and staying in many of the prominent cities on the South Pacific coast. From time to time affectionate letters reached his family and friends in England, dated at the various places where he stopped during his wanderings. On the 20th of April, 1854, he sailed from Rio in a ship called the *Bella*, which foundered at sea, and was treated by the owners and underwriters as lost. A Chancery suit was instituted, in which his death was legally proved. Year after year rolled by; his cousin KATE, to whom he had been engaged, married Mr. RADCLIFFE; his father died, and his death was widely published; but nothing was heard of the son until the plaintiff set up his claim.

The claimant's case is that he is ROGER TICHBORNE; that he was picked up at sea with several of the seamen, and carried to Melbourne; but of this there has been no other evidence than his own statement.

In 1862 he was at Wagga-Wagga, Australia, where he was occupied with horses, slaughtering, etc. There he formed the acquaintance of a man named GIBBES, through whom the conspiracy, if such it was, is thought to have been arranged.

In 1865 Lady TICHBORNE saw in the London *Times* the advertisement of a "Missing Friends' Office" in Sydney, to which she transmitted a description of her long-lost son; and it is the theory of the defense that unscrupulous parties, to secure the reward promised for his discovery,

Top right: The Tichborne Claimant, Andrew J. Garvey. Top left: The real Sir Roger Tichborne. Below is the shack he is said to have lived in in Wagga Wagga, New South Wales, Australia.

Dartmoor Prison lay dormant and empty until 1850. Now that convicts could no longer be sent to the United States and transportation to Australia was also coming to an end, British prisons and hulks once again began to overflow. Queen Victoria's husband, Prince Albert, suggested that Dartmoor could be used as a civil prison. Inmates could quarry granite and reclaim some of the moorland for farming.

The old dormitories were converted into single-cell accommodations. Many of the early arrivals were from a hospital prison and were treated quite gently. Discipline was lax, but gradually, all the country's worst offenders were transferred to Dartmoor. The regime became harsher. Solitary confinement was put to use, and the rule of silence was imported from the United States. Working parties were sent out to break rocks with hammers or to dig the bogs in a line abreast, sometimes up to their knees in water. Luckier prisoners and the less-able worked inside, making uniforms for **warders** and police officers, wooden doors and windows for the warders' accommodations, and metal gates, posts, and wheels for the prison and farm.

Gradually, fields emerged and the farm was stocked with sheep, pigs, cattle, and horses. Many of the prisoners from the city had never seen a live sheep or cow before, yet farm work was popular and the prison began to win prizes at local agricultural shows. Later, during World War I, many of the prison inmates were allowed to enlist in the fighting forces. Their places at Dartmoor were taken by 1,000 "conchies" (conscientious objectors) who did not believe in taking part in war. A field they had once tilled became known as "Conchies Field."

THE TICHBORNE CLAIMANT

A little color was brought to the prison in 1874 with the arrival of the Tichborne Claimant, whose trial had been one of the most sensational of the time. Back in 1853, young Sir Roger Charles Tichborne had left England for South America. However, the vessel on which he was sailing onward from Buenos Aires to Jamaica never arrived and was presumed lost. His mother, Lady Tichborne, refused to believe that he was dead. She went to great lengths to find him, even advertising in newspapers worldwide.

She was overjoyed when she heard from Sydney, Australia, that a man from the small town of Wagga Wagga answered Roger's description and was claiming to be her long-lost son. In fact, he turned out to be a stout man remarkably dissimilar to the slim Roger, coarse in speech and ignorant of the French language in which Roger had been fluent.

Nonetheless, he was accepted, first by two old family servants (the fortune at stake was a large one), from whom he learned something of the family history, and then by the lonely Lady Tichborne. Roger's mother had a limited income and no provision had been made for her in the family estate, which had been left to an infant. She may have hoped her "son" would be more generous.

The rest of the family was less convinced that the man was Roger. When Lady Tichborne died, they brought a civil case, claiming that the fellow was, in fact, Arthur Orton, a butcher from Wapping (in London's East End), who had jumped ship at Valparaiso in 1850 and then made his way to Australia.

The case began on May 11, 1871, and lasted 100 days. Many people swore that the man from Wagga Wagga was Roger Tichborne, but the jury found for the family and the claimant was arrested and charged with **perjury**. The jury in that trial also decided he was not Roger Tichborne. They found him guilty on two counts of perjury, and he was sentenced to 14 years penal servitude. However, many hard-bitten old **lags** at Dartmoor did believe his claim. They thought he was a gentleman, and a wise one at that. Fellow prisoner Michael Davitt, an Irishman serving 15 years for treason-felony, wrote in his *Prison Diary*:

"Sir Roger soon became the recognized authority upon every matter of moment to the 1,000 citizens of Dartmoor's criminal population, from the merits of the skilly to the evils of trial by jury.... "

SHERLOCK ON THE MOORS

In *The Hound of the Baskervilles,* Sherlock Holmes (here played by Tom Baker in one of many television adaptions) and Dr. Watson see armed soldiers and prison officers out searching for an escaped prisoner. Selden, the ferocious "Notting Hill Murderer," had been "out for three days" and was, they were told, likely to cut the throat of anyone who came across him.

"It needed but this," reported Dr. Watson, "to complete the grim suggestiveness of the barren waste, the chilling wind and the darkling sky. Even Baskerville fell silent and pulled his overcoat more closely around him."

A guard in Dartmoor Prison, photographed in 1969, checks a prisoner through a peephole in a door. At the time, questions were being asked about prison security following the escape of Frank Mitchell.

THE DARTMOOR MUTINY

Outside working parties offered opportunities for impulsive escape attempts, which were not always a good idea. A man named Brown, who ran off during a blizzard in February 1853, had to have his toes amputated due to frostbite. However, there were some successful escapes from the prison, which was described by inmates as "halfway to hell." Later, in 1928, came the "first motorcar escape." A convict got out of the prison building wearing a prison officer's jacket and using a skeleton key he had made. He found his way to the house of Father Finnegan, the local Roman Catholic priest, donned his clerical garb, and borrowed his car. He was far away before the escape was discovered and enjoyed a couple of days' freedom in the resort of Paignton before he was caught.

On a far more serious note, undoubtedly the most dramatic event in the history of Dartmoor Prison was the 1932 mutiny, which was supposedly sparked off by watery porridge and a variety of other **grievances**. Leading the revolt were some of the tougher types now arriving on the moor, such as the "motor bandits" or gangsters.

While the crimes British gangsters committed were nowhere near the scale or drama of their American counterparts, they could be ruthless and occasionally carried pistols when out robbing and breaking into safes.

The mutinously rampant prisoners slashed the faces of two of the guards and then ran riot in a frenzy of destruction. They set fire to the administration block and assaulted and poured porridge over the head of a visiting Home Office official. At first, the prison officers were helpless, because not only were they heavily outnumbered, but they were also unarmed. (Only guards on duty at night were regularly armed.)

THE CRAZY AX-MAN

The most famous escape from Dartmoor came on December 12, 1966, when crazy ax-man Frank Mitchell was sprung from a trustee working party by gangster Ronnie Kray. Mitchell was not really crazy—just a bit simple—and it was his criminal colleague who had once carried an ax.

Kray rescued Mitchell from Dartmoor partly because he felt sorry for the man, who did seem to have had a bit of a raw deal, and partly because it would make him look big in the underworld. As it turned out, Mitchell became something of a liability. He was drawing too much heat from the police, and so the Kray brothers had him murdered.

THE PRISON OFFICERS FIGHT BACK

Eventually, rifles were distributed to prison officers, who ringed the outer perimeter, which kept the prisoners inside. Reinforcements arrived in the form of the local police, who went in with batons swinging, and order was restored. Thirty-one mutineers stood trial at a special local court, extra sentences were handed out to the ringleaders, and questions were asked about the running of the prison and bad behavior of the warders.

It is always difficult to decide who is telling the truth in these matters. Those deprived of their freedom and living in uncomfortable surroundings treasure their privileges and can become obsessed with the minutiae of their limited lives. There is also the problem that telling lies is part of a criminal's "job description." Also, many of the truly hardened inmates are difficult to keep in order. On the other hand, it is true that some of those in charge abuse the power they are given over others.

Whatever the truth of the matter, improvements in prison life were

IT IS NO FUN FOR THE WARDERS EITHER

Dartmoor's cells were dark and damp. Prisoners rose at 5:30 A.M. and went to church every day at 7:00 A.M. The lights were put out at 8:00 P.M. Once a week, the prisoners bathed in a communal bathhouse. However, the place was no more popular with the warders and their families, whose houses, too, were damp and dismal. And there was little to do in the village of Princetown, which had grown up around the prison walls. Even today, Princetown is described in the current *Rough Guide to Britain* as having "a somewhat oppressed air."

Matters improved slightly in 1883 with the coming of the Great Western Railway branch line, on which families could escape to the lively port of Plymouth.

made. A further riot took place at Dartmoor and several other prisons across Britain in 1990. Again, an enormous amount of damage was done, and this time, an inmate was killed. Today, as with many old prisons around the world, there is talk of closing Dartmoor, and it was recently decided to limit the intake to category C (low-risk) prisoners.

"Mad" Frankie Frazer, who had a reputation for enormous physical strength (as well as brutality), is led away by prison officers after an unsuccessful escape attempt from an institution for the criminally insane. He was later sent to Dartmoor.

The Big House—San Quentin State Penitentiary, California

The most striking thing about the peach-colored fortress of San Quentin is its spectacular position on the edge of the Marin Peninsula north of San Francisco. From a distance, it might almost be an expensive resort complex. However, its 6,000 inmates are not able to appreciate the wonderful sea views—they see only the sky. Hurriedly established as a response to the 1848–1849 Gold Rush, which included many of the lawless among its hopeful prospectors, San Quentin is the oldest penitentiary in the state of California.

LIVING IN SAN QUENTIN PENITENTIARY

Prison life begins with being admitted. Admission into most prisons follows the same humiliating pattern, and San Quentin is no different. Prisoners are made to strip naked, **orifices** are examined to ensure that no forbidden substances, such as drugs, are brought in, and then prisoners get in line for a prison uniform. Being involuntarily naked in front of others makes you feel vulnerable and does not do much for your dignity.

As with many such 19th-century prisons, early conditions at "The Big House" (a slang term for prison) were harsh, unsanitary, and unhealthy.

Left: Cell 33, on Death Row, San Quentin Penitentiary, in 1969. The cell had just been made ready to hold Sirhan Sirhan, the killer of Robert F. Kennedy. His sentence was later commuted to one of life imprisonment.

This photograph shows an older section of San Quentin in 1934. Before the prison was built in 1854, inmates were incarcerated on prison ships. Women inmates were moved out of San Quentin in 1927.

Most cells had no lavatories, only buckets. The inmates had to empty them in the morning, a process known as "slopping out" or "emptying the honey bucket." This situation continued well into the late 20th century in prisons in the United States and elsewhere, and in some places continues today.

San Quentin has always been the venue of most of California's executions. Initially, these were by hanging. The last of these took place in 1936, when Rattlesnake James went to the gallows. He stuck his wife's foot in a box of rattlesnakes, but when that proved ineffective, held her head under water until she drowned.

After that, the gas chamber took over. As with the electric chair, death

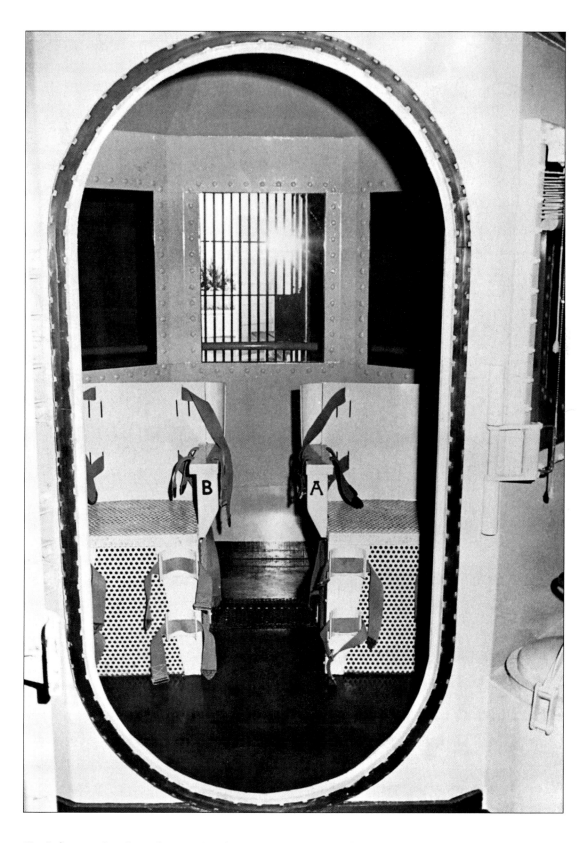

The infamous San Quentin gas chamber, photographed in 1974. Up to 1967, 194 people were executed there, including Caryl Chessman and three women.

A prisoners classroom at San Quentin in 1934. Even before the advent of reforming warden Clinton T. Duffy in 1940, attempts were made to occupy and educate inmates, and in doing so, to help rehabilitate them.

by gassing was thought to offer a more humane alternative to hanging. The first execution by gas (obtained by pouring sulfuric acid onto pellets of sodium cyanide contained in a bowl under the victim's chair) took place in 1924. Ten states set up gas chambers, but it was San Quentin that was to become symbolic of the method.

Like most U.S. prisons, San Quentin became involved in war work. Down the years, it had produced furniture, shoes, harnesses, wagons, and **jute**—mostly jute. During World War II, the prisoners built assault craft for the Army and assembled ration books for distribution to civilians.

WARDEN DUFFY

The 1940s brought two major changes to this huge penitentiary. Workshop production changed, and Warden Duffy arrived. Clinton T. Duffy (the son of a San Quentin guard) was a progressive thinker and held the position of warden at San Quentin from 1940–1954. The changes he brought were far-reaching. He improved the food, curtailed harsh punishment and brutality by the guards, and introduced more opportunities for education, hobbies, sports, and entertainment. He also created an Inmate Representative Committee with elected officers, who, he hoped would replace the gangster prison "bosses" who had ruled before. Duffy also wrote a book called *88 Men and Two Women* in which he gave a description of death in the gas chamber. Initially, he claimed, there would be extreme evidence of horror, pain, and suffocation, but in a matter of seconds, the prisoner would become unconscious. (In 1996, lethal injection began to be offered as an alternative.)

Nineteen-year-old Edward Bunker was in solitary confinement in San Quentin State Penitentiary when a prisoner in the nearby Death Row sent him a copy of *Argosy* magazine. Emblazoned on the cover were details of their lead feature—an excerpt from the book, *Cell 2455, Death Row*—by this very prisoner, Caryl Chessman. Bunker was stunned. This man, he thought, is on Death Row. What difference could publication make to him? If it were me, it would change my life. As Bunker was later to write in *Mr. Blue*: "Suddenly, with a force of revelation, I said aloud: 'Why not me?'" Of course, there is nothing new about prisoners writing books on their experiences.

And according to Sing Sing warden Lewis E. Lawes, almost every one of

CARYL CHESSMAN

Born in 1922, Caryl Chessman was sentenced to death in 1948 after he was convicted on 17 charges of kidnapping, robbery, and rape. He conducted a brilliant legal battle, resulting in eight stays of execution, amounting to what was then a record of 12 years under sentence of death without reprieve.

While in prison, he learned four languages and wrote and published three books: *Cell 2455, Death Row* (1956), *Trial by Ordeal* (1956), and *The Face of Justice* (1958). There was a public outcry in the U.S. and around the world when he eventually went to the gas chamber at San Quentin in 1960.

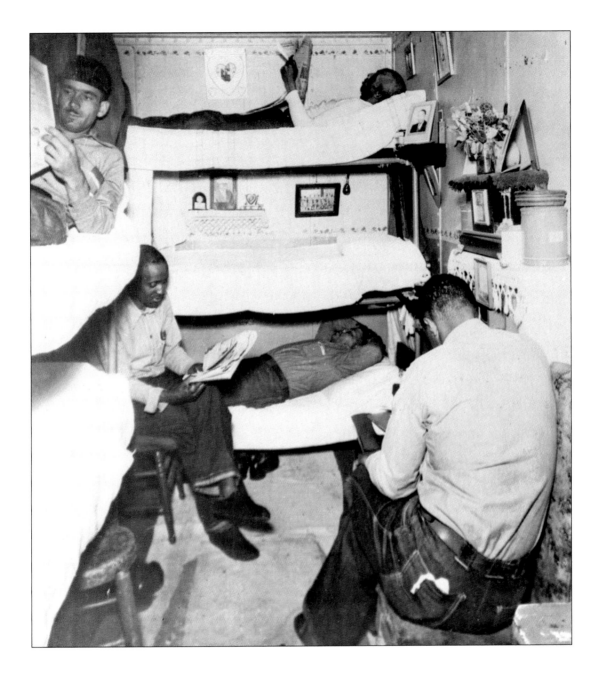

A typical scene from a cell in an old San Quentin block shows how overcrowded the prison had become in 1935. Although measuring only 11 feet, 8 inches by 7 feet, 8 inches (3.5 by 2.3 m), it housed five prisoners, and the only toilet facilities were a single bucket.

them thinks his story is worth telling. As Lawes writes in *Twenty Thousand Years in Sing Sing* (1932), "No sooner is he settled into his cell after his admission into the prison, then he sharpens his pencil, somehow obtains a pad, and is at it."

In most of the books that were actually finished, he noticed that inmates usually blamed their downfall on a woman—"the siren, blonde, or dark-haired vixen"—for whom they had stolen to provide luxuries.

THE STORY OF EDWARD BUNKER

Edward Bunker arrived in San Quentin in 1952, aged 17, having been convicted on a charge of assault with a deadly weapon. He had already met the captain of the guard, Red Nelson, in the earlier stages of his youthful criminal career. (Most prisoners see little of the wardens because it is the captains of the guard who have day-to-day control.)

Nelson, known as "tough but fair," had told Bunker he was not as tough as he thought he was. The lad would be "but a pimple on the asses of the guys at Alcatraz." The captain described how he had been one of the guards locked in the cell with six others "while three bad-ass bank robbers from Oklahoma and Kentucky" emptied a .45 into it—he escaped without injury. "It made him somehow fearless," said Bunker.

The jute mill had just burned down when Bunker arrived, which left him and 300 other prisoners without work, so he was free to wander the vast prison, making lots of friends en route. He worked out in the gym, took part in bouts in the boxing room, and traded with a dental assistant, who ran his own business making crowns and bridgework, not catered for by the state, but paid for by the cons with cigarettes, money, or marijuana. He also visited the Death Row cook, who was allowed to make steak and egg sandwiches from leftovers for friends or for sale—a welcome change from the dreadful regular prison food.

At 4:00 P.M., 4,000 working prisoners would be released into The Big Yard, a canyon between the cellblocks, which was, Bunker discovered, invariably cold and windy. Just after 6:00 P.M., those not attending evening classes, gym, or choir practice would be locked up for the night. However, Bunker preferred staying in his cell where he could continue reading and, following the inspiration of Chessman, get down to writing his novel.

WANTED: ONE FAIRY GODMOTHER

Along his deprived and criminal path, Bunker had acquired a "fairy godmother," Mrs. Louise Wallis, wife of Hal Wallis, the movie mogul. She sent him a portable typewriter. To pay for a correspondence course in English, Bunker sold some of his blood.

In common with all the large prisons holding long-termers, San Quentin was clearly a violent place with continuous grave risk of severe injury or death. Bunker discovered that there was no prison boss among the convicts of the sort so often portrayed in movies. The only way to protect yourself was to show you stood for

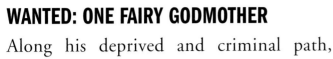

Edward Bunker, who played Mr. Blue in Quentin Tarantino's movie *Reservoir Dogs*, lounges in a leather jacket. He began writing while in prison and eventually made a new life for himself.

no messing and were prepared to knife someone first, if necessary. Also, it was best not to make unnecessary enemies and to become part of a group whose members lent each other protection. Bunker became part of several, but he was still stabbed once and had his face slashed "from temple to lip by a cell partner I had been bullying."

For a while, Ed Bunker's best friend was Leon, "the most intelligent man I'd met in prison." Leon was an African American. At that time, a form of segregation was in place in many U.S. prisons. In fact, in 1953, white

WRITTEN OFF

One day in 1937, Warden Johnston of Alcatraz was chatting with a guard in the dining hall when a young prisoner named Whitey Phillips bolted from the lineup and crashed his fist behind the warden's right ear. As Johnston dropped unconscious, Phillips kicked his head and rained hammer blows on the man's face.

The prisoner's action was thought to be the result of harsh discipline following a recent prisoner revolt about conditions, but, as described in *Escape from Alcatraz,* it turned out that there was a deeper reason.

Phillips, at first bitter about the rather harsh sentence he had received for his misdeeds, began to pull himself around and write a book about the Rock. Having heard that Warden Johnston had recently had a book published (*Prison Life is Different,* 1937), he asked Johnston whether he would like to look it over and make any criticisms. Weeks went by with no response. When Phillips eventually saw the warden again he asked hopefully, "What did you think of my book?" Johnston replied, "I read that manuscript and decided it was not the kind of material you should have, so I confiscated it."

Alcatraz prisoners almost rioted until segregation was enforced. Bunker found, however, that in his first incarceration at San Quentin, the race issue was not a huge problem.

When Bunker returned in the 1960s (following **parole** violations that included armed robbery), he found it was an entirely different story. Hard drugs were rife, and the race war raged both outside and inside the prison. Inside was much more dangerous because even if you wished to, you could not escape confrontation.

RADICAL POLITICAL THINKERS IN PRISON

George Jackson's young criminal career, like that of Edward Bunker, culminated in graduation from youth correction centers to an adult prison. He entered Soledad in 1961 at the age of 19. Racial discrimination had already made George Jackson feel aggrieved, and his anger was further stoked by the feeling that he had been deceived into pleading guilty to a relatively minor charge (robbing a gas station) in the hope of a lighter sentence. Instead, due to his record, he had received an indefinite sentence of one year in prison to life. In 1962, he was transferred to San Quentin, where he met W.L. Nolen, who introduced him to the work of leading radical political thinkers, such as Karl Marx and Mao Tse-tung. From then on, Jackson channeled his energies into thoughts of a black revolution. He helped form the prison's Black Guerrilla Family (BGF) and, later, the prison branch of the Black Panthers.

Continually refused parole, Jackson was transferred back to Soledad, where, in 1970, five African-American prisoners attacked two white convicts. In the chaos, three African-American prisoners were shot dead by guards. A few days later, a young white Soledad guard died when he was beaten and thrown from the third tier onto the concrete below. Jackson and two others were charged with his murder.

Well-known liberals and radicals took up Jackson's case. Two in particular were an African-American professor at the University of

California, Angela Davis, and a lawyer named Fay Stender. Stender edited his prison letters, which were published under the title *Soledad Brother* (1970). The book became a bestseller. George Jackson became famous, and he and the other accused were dubbed the "Soledad Brothers." Meanwhile, African-American prisoners murdered the officer who was guarding an African-American witness in the case against them, on the mistaken assumption that he had the key to the witness's room.

PENITENTIARY RACE WARS

On August, 7, 1970, Jackson's brother, Jonathan, burst into a Marin County courtroom, freed three prisoners, and took hostage Judge Harold Haley and the deputy district attorney. His intention was to exchange the hostages for his brother George, now back in San Quentin. In the shoot-out that followed, two inmates and Jonathan Jackson were killed. The judge (who had been booby-trapped with a wire around his neck attached to a shotgun trigger) had his head blown off, and the deputy district attorney's spine was severed, leaving him a paraplegic.

Then the interracial carnage began in California's prisons. African-American prisoners began stabbing, slashing, and killing white prisoners and guards—because they were white and therefore the oppressors—and the whites retaliated.

As Bunker points out in *Mr. Blue*, for two decades, no guards had been killed in a California prison, but within a few months, a dozen were murdered by African-American prisoners in Folsom, Soledad, and San Quentin. The number of inmates who died appears to have been countless. Meanwhile, George Jackson became more famous and was continuously interviewed by the foreign and U.S. press. He published another book of essays and letters called *Blood in My Eye* (1971), in which he called for revolution and predicted his own murder in prison. In fact, it was on August 21, 1971, that Jackson was shot dead after he and other African Americans killed three guards and two trustee inmates.

The San Quentin Six, charged with murder after a 1971 escape attempt. Top, from left to right, Fleeta Drumgo, Hugo Pinell, and Luis Talamantez. Bottom, from left to right, John Larry Spain, David Johnson, and Willie Tait.

The story ended happily for Edward Bunker. After 17 years of writing (six books and countless short stories), his novel, *No Beast So Fierce*, was accepted for publication—as was his feature on prison race wars by *Harper's Magazine*. Coincidentally, I was on the British Crime Writers' Association Non-Fiction panel, which awarded *Mr. Blue* the Gold Dagger for the year 2000.

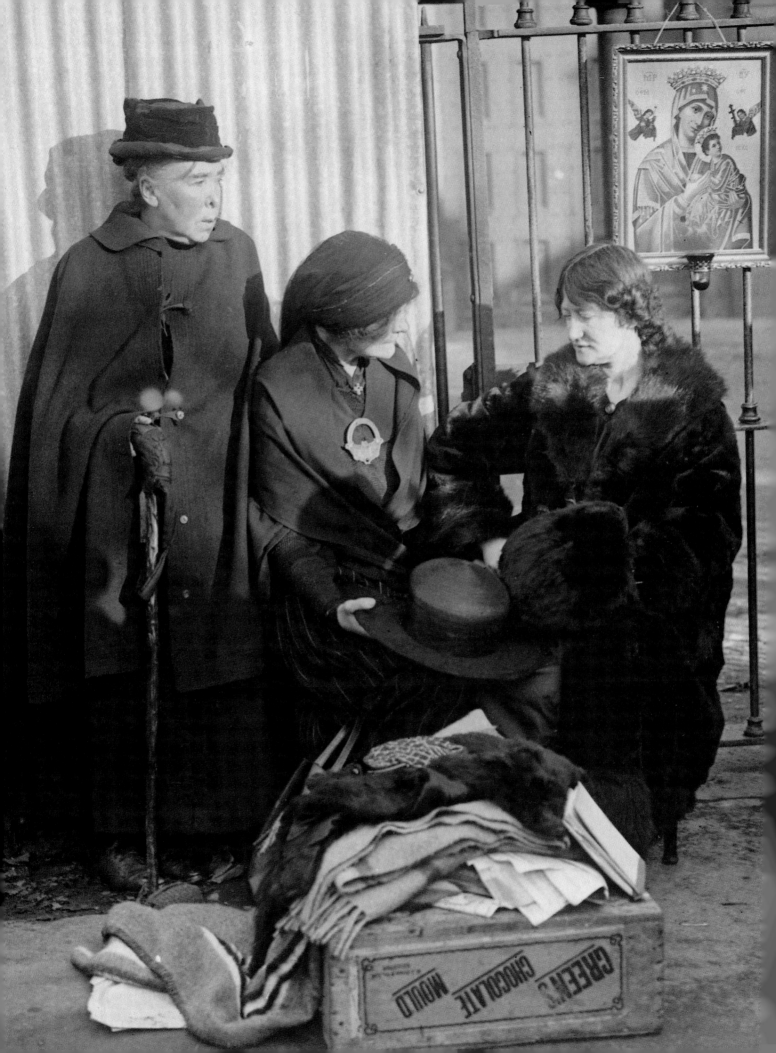

Ireland's Model Prison— Mountjoy, Dublin

Mountjoy, also called "The Joy," is named after the family who owned the land on which it was built. Renowned as a prison where political prisoners were incarcerated during the Irish War of Independence, it is also the venue of several prison curiosities. For example, Sean Kavanagh, Mountjoy's longest-serving governor, was a former inmate. And the first prisoners to go on a hunger strike in cells of "The Joy" were not Irish freedom fighters, as you might expect, but English suffragettes—women struggling to be allowed the right to vote. Then there is the fact that in the early days, there were more women incarcerated at Mountjoy than in any other prison in the world. The most acute danger they faced was not violence, but the threat of insanity.

THE SILENT AND SEPARATE SYSTEM

This was the direct result of the "silent and separate system" imported from the U.S. and taken up and honed by the designers of Pentonville Prison in London. In fact, Mountjoy Prison was an almost exact replica of Pentonville, and there is no doubt that the Pentonville Model Prison was

Left: This photograph shows supporters of Sinn Fein hunger strikers outside Mountjoy in 1922— Mrs Maud MacBride, Miss Barry Delaney, and Miss Annie MacSwiney. Maud's husband, John, was executed as a rebel in 1916.

Fenian prisoners exercising under close guard at Mountjoy Prison in 1866. Their large-scale imprisonment there had begun the previous year. More than 60 passed through Mountjoy up to 1868.

considered to be the ultimate in penal building and reform. People came from far and wide to view its wonders, and the design was much copied.

People who supported the silent and separate policy sincerely thought they were doing the right thing by ridding prisons of the filth, mayhem, and danger to physical health suffered when inmates were crammed in together. Also, they felt they were helping prisoners reform by giving them the opportunity for quiet contemplation while preventing them from being contaminated by fellow inmates.

Opened on March 27, 1850, the four wings of Mountjoy Prison radiated out from a central hub. Each of the 496 cells was large, measuring 13 by 7 feet (4 by 2 m) and offering such luxuries as ceramic flushing toilets and self-regulating central heating. The cell door had a one-way spy hole for the warder and a hatch through which food was passed three times a day. High up on the outside wall was a small window, but it was glazed with fluted glass to save the prisoner from the distraction of glimpsing the outside world.

The prisoners were kept continually busy in their cells, making clothes, shoes, and mats or weaving linen or wool cloth. Silence and separation continued during their daily hour of exercise, while at church they sat in high-walled booths, as well as at morning school, where they were taught to read and write. The high-walled booths were a significant innovation, but were to come under much pressure from the need to maintain a high work output.

Writing of Irish convict reform in 1863, Charles B. Gibson referred to Mountjoy as "a most beautiful piece of prison machinery." The trouble was, all the splendid design did not compensate for the unbearable solitude, and the beautiful machinery did not work.

THE REALITY BEHIND THE SYSTEM

As Tim Carey points out in his book, *Mountjoy: The Story of a Prison*, the convicts sweated profusely at their labors. The cell toilets were frequently blocked or misused "by men ignorant of such contraptions," the gas lighting (at that time a hissing flame) smelled and starved the air of oxygen, and much of the prisoners' employment called for the use of toxic chemicals. The result was that when the cell door hatch was opened, a putrid mix of smells rushed out.

Prisoners began breaking their cell windows so they could breathe some fresh air, and it became necessary to install louvered windows that they could control themselves. Then, in 1854, the Irish prison authorities decided that work was too much of a pleasant distraction for men who were meant to be contemplating their sins, so it ceased, apart from some voluntary oakum picking. This was one of the most soul-destroying and unpleasant occupations possible, involving picking strands out of old tarred ropes so that they could be used to make new ropes.

In 1858, a women's wing was completed. However, unlike the men, who, after nine months good behavior could transfer to an intermediate prison where associated labor was permitted, the women were obliged to serve out their full sentences at Mountjoy. As a concession, after four months isolation, they were allowed to leave their cell doors open.

Nonetheless, many women prisoners rapidly became depressed, suffered from attacks of hysteria, or developed paranoia. Almost three percent were actually diagnosed clinically insane. They were required to work, but the authorities were obliged to vary employment from the constant knitting and sewing, and improve the diet, which was deliberately kept limited and boring.

Irish freedom fighters began appearing at Mountjoy in 1865, and by 1868, 60 **Fenians** convicted of treason felony had passed through on their way to penal servitude in English prisons. Many more were held without trial, to be eventually released on the condition that they emigrated.

The next big influx was the 30 Invincibles (an offshoot organization of the Fenians), who were arrested for the assassination of the new Chief Secretary for Ireland, Lord Frederick Cavendish, and Permanent Under Secretary, T.H. Burke, in Phoenix Park in May 1882. Five Invincibles were sentenced to death and the rest given penal servitude, but most of the latter were released from Mountjoy in 1891.

This illustration shows Fenian prisoners marched out of Dublin Castle on their way to Mountjoy Prison in 1867. Many would go on to serve their sentences for treason on mainland Britain.

WOMEN'S SUFFRAGE

While the Irish were fighting for home rule, it became apparent to women that this freedom was not going to extend to them. At that time, there were only limited economic opportunities for women, and in those early days, the numbers of Irish women in prison (more than one-third of the total prison population) was much higher than in the rest of Europe (10–20 percent) or the United States (about four percent). This was due, Tim Carey claims, to the limited options for women in Ireland: wife, domestic servant, thief, or prostitute.

To make matters worse, the home rule bills coming before Parliament contained no provision for female suffrage (the right to vote). In protest over this, four Irish suffragettes (Kathleen Houston, Margaret Hasler, Hilda Webb, and Maud Lloyd) broke the windows of various government buildings on June 13, 1912. As a result, they were sentenced to six months in Mountjoy.

Six days later, three English suffragettes (Mary Leigh, Gladys Evans, and a Mrs. Baines) were arrested after setting fire to the curtains of a box in the Theatre Royal, Dublin. Prime Minister Asquith was due to speak at a home rule meeting in the theater the following day, so the Englishwomen wanted to demonstrate their solidarity with their Irish sisters.

This was not Mary Leigh's first arrest. She had begun the window-breaking campaign in London in 1909 by smashing those of the prime minister's residence at 10 Downing Street. However, arson was a more serious offense than breaking windows or holding illegal demonstrations. Although the Dublin judge admitted that he found Mary Leigh to be a remarkable lady, she and Evans were sentenced to five years penal servitude, while Mrs. Baines received seven months hard labor. Once inside Mountjoy, the women went on a hunger strike, demanding that they be treated as political prisoners and be given a pledge that votes for women would be included in the home rule bill. These demands were refused, and the women were force-fed.

English suffragettes celebrating the release of two of their number from Holloway Prison in London. Mary Leigh and Edith New were imprisoned for smashing the prime minister's windows at 10 Downing Street, London.

FIGHTING BACK BY SELF-STARVATION

Force-feeding involves fluid being poured down a funnel through a rubber tube into the stomach. It is extremely unpleasant and can be dangerous. Mrs. Leigh vomited back much of what had been forced down her throat and lost almost 28 pounds (12.7 kg) of weight.

Suffragette reinforcements arrived from London to help distribute thousands of black-edged leaflets and posters announcing, "Three Women are Facing Death in Mountjoy." They also helped with a demonstration in Phoenix Park, which was attended by thousands. Fearful that the women might die, the authorities released them. Many more suffragettes were to go on hunger strikes in Mountjoy before the start of World War I, when women's suffrage hostilities ceased for the duration.

Then came another issue altogether: following the Easter Rising of 1916, the leaders were executed in Kilmainham Gaol, while Mountjoy once again acted as a clearing house for over 100 political prisoners en route to

A militant suffragette is arrested in London in 1912, probably for window breaking after efforts to gain the vote had once again been thwarted by Prime Minister Herbert Asquith.

England to serve their sentences. These included Eamon de Valera, who was later to become the Irish prime minister, and Countess Markiewicz, who had been sentenced to death for her part in the Easter Rising, but was reprieved. She was later to become a notable politician. By 1917, most of these were back in Ireland.

That year, Sinn Fein prisoners in Mountjoy began a hunger strike and on its fifth day, one of them, Thomas Ashe, died while he was being force-fed. The authorities claimed he suffered from heart failure and congestion of the lungs, but the occurrence reignited the revolutionary fuse. Sinn Fein prisoners adopted a policy of noncooperation. Cells were trashed, bedlam reigned at night, and every opportunity was taken for confrontation. While the War of Independence raged (1919–1921), the prison staff was in an unenviable position. Despite

often being in sympathy with the political aims of the prisoners, they were obliged to try to enforce the rules. They were also aware that the Sinn Fein could be dangerous enemies and, the way things were going, these prisoners might soon be taking over and becoming their bosses.

Escapes became frequent and, in 1920, 92 prisoners began a hunger strike. All eyes were on Mountjoy. A general strike was called in support of the prisoners. The authorities no longer dared to attempt force-feeding and had to give in and release them.

MOUNTJOY: THE POLITICAL PRISON

Another general strike was called on March 14, 1921, when six men were hanged at Mountjoy. These were Frank Flood, Patrick Doyle, Thomas Bryan, and Bernard Ryan, who had been found armed with explosives and firearms, and Thomas Whelan and Patrick Moran, convicted of the murders of 11 British intelligence agents. (They protested their innocence.) Shortly after, on June 7, two more Sinn Fein members were hanged for the murder of a police sergeant. However, even after the signing of the Anglo-Irish Treaty on December 6, 1921, the executions did not cease. Republicans believed that Michael Collins had sold them out by agreeing to the British retention of the six counties now known as Northern Ireland, Consequently, fighting and political killings continued.

Once again, Mountjoy filled up with political prisoners, but this time they were anti-treaty combatants from the Irish Civil War. Michael Collins, by then head of the provisional government, and his deputy, Sean Hales, were assassinated and 70 Irish Republican Army (IRA) prisoners shot in various Irish prisons. Several of the anti-treaty leaders met their deaths in Mountjoy. In 1923, the anti-treaty forces called for a permanent cessation of hostilities, and, in 1924, a much-damaged Mountjoy became a civilian prison once again.

The separate and silent system was abandoned in Britain in the early 1920s on the grounds that, rather than leading to finer thoughts, it

Irish republican volunteers stand outside the General Post Office in Dublin soon after the Easter Rising in Dublin, April 1916. After the rising failed, many of those captured by the British were imprisoned in Mountjoy.

An illustration from the French *La Petite Journal,* October 28, 1923, of hunger strikers at Mountjoy refusing hot food. The fatal, 74-day fast of Terence MacSwiney in 1921 aroused worldwide sympathy.

THE PRISON PLAYWRIGHT

One prisoner who added to Mountjoy's fame was playwright and IRA supporter, Brendan Behan. He was imprisoned there on three occasions and, like Edward Bunker in San Quentin, used his time inside to good effect.

Behan's first visit was for a few days in March 1942, following his release from an English reformatory, where he had been held for trying to blow up a Liverpool dockyard. Shortly after his release from Mountjoy, he was back again, having been sentenced to 14 years of penal servitude for the attempted murder of two detectives. His initial 14 months were served at Mountjoy, where he wrote his first play *The Landlady*. It was to be staged by the prisoners, but, during rehearsals, disputes broke out over the play's bad language, and the project had to be abandoned. Behan's best-known plays are *The Hostage* and *The Quare Fellow*. The latter is set in Mountjoy at the time of the execution of an inmate for the murder of his own brother.

Behan was released from Mountjoy during an amnesty for IRA members at the end of World War II. However, he returned there in 1948 after assaulting a policeman and using obscene language. He was back again, in 1954, for being drunk and disorderly. He died in 1964.

Sympathizers outside Mountjoy Prison waving to Sinn Fein member, Thomas Traynor, as he is led to his execution for the murder of a British cadet soldier in 1921. Mountjoy became home to numerous political prisoners in this period.

promoted morbid and introspective tendencies, suicide, or sullen, morose, and revengeful feelings. Interestingly, Quakers were among those who campaigned for its cessation. Some of them had been imprisoned as conscientious objectors during the war and were horrified by what they experienced. This was not, they declared, what the Quakers of Philadelphia had intended when they promoted the systems that led to the building of the Eastern State Penitentiary all those years before. In 1934, the system was abolished in Ireland, but apparently old lags found it difficult to break the habit of speaking furtively out of the corners of their twisted mouths.

MOUNTJOY TODAY

In 1991, the Mountjoy Visiting Committee issued a damning report on the prison, declaring it to be grossly overcrowded, the conditions scandalous and far below European standards. One curious anomaly revealed was that the suicide rate in Irish prisons (but chiefly in Mountjoy) was double the English rate per capita in prisons and triple that of Scotland. Another concern, which might have raised a wry smile among early inmates, was that, due to overcrowding, inmates were placed in multiple cells and so deprived of their privacy. A major redevelopment program is now in the process of improving Ireland's prisons, including Mountjoy.

The number of women in Ireland's penal institutions fell dramatically over the years, and by the year 2000 was down to three percent of the total prison population. Those at the Mountjoy complex are fortunate in that they are to occupy the state's first custom-built women's prison, the Dochas Centre, which received a Special Merit prize in the Millennium Construction Excellence Awards.

Going Around in Circles—Stateville Penitentiary, Joliet, Illinois

During the early 19th century, three architectural prison styles evolved: the Eastern, the Auburn, and the panopticon. The Eastern, as in Eastern State Penitentiary in Philadelphia, featured long blocks of cells radiating out from a central rotunda. Within these blocks, large, single-story cells lined the outside walls. Auburn Prison introduced the idea of long blocks, within which cells were stacked back-to-back along the center, with corridors running along the outside of these. The soulless, six-story blocks at Sing Sing were among the longest of these blocks ever built. The third style was the panopticon, designed by English philosopher and scholar, Jeremy Bentham, in 1791. The most imposing of these panopticon prisons is the huge Stateville Penitentiary built in 1919 at Joliet, in Illinois.

THE EVOLVING STYLES OF PRISON ARCHITECTURE

Prison ideas passed back and forth across the Atlantic. Several European prisons were built on the panopticon design, and some, like Stateville,

Left: This is one of the many enclosed guard stations that stand at the center of the circular cell blocks at Stateville Penitentiary. From here, all the cells and their corridors are in view.

appeared in the United States. Panopticon prison blocks are circular. The cells line the outside walls and radiate around a central hub containing an enclosed guards' station. Bentham thought that this design would make supervision easier and that instructions or sermons could be issued to all from the central point. Also, he thought that the prisoners, realizing they could always be observed, would be more likely to behave themselves and reflect on their crimes.

The industrial city of Joliet, just west of Chicago, was already home to a large state prison that carried its name. Built in the late 1850s, Joliet Penitentiary, like many Victorian prisons, resembles a Gothic castle or fortress. Inside, it was run along Auburn lines. Prisoners were silent, but not separated, and they wore striped uniforms, walked in lockstep wearing chains around their ankles, and were subject to harsh discipline.

The city was named after 17th-century French-Canadian explorer Louis Joliet. Unlike Sing Sing, which changed its name to Ossining in 1901 to rid its goods of the stigma of the prison, Joliet has kept the name of its founder despite having two large penitentiaries in its midst. Now, Joliet Prison is closing. During its final years, it has operated as a reception and classification center for northern Illinois while retaining a permanent core of around 250, mostly long-term, prisoners. "Nobody would build a prison like this now," Warden Ron Matrisciano told *Chicago Sun Times* crime reporter, Frank Main. "It's too staff-intensive and there are a lot of blind spots." This was an opinion echoed by Californian Correctional Agency spokesman, Steve Green, when talking to *USA Today* reporter John Ritter about the proposed closing of San Quentin: "There are all kinds of nooks and crannies where inmates can hide. Modern prisons have absolute line-of-sight everywhere."

A new 1,800-bed reception and classification center costing $90 million is being built at Stateville, now referred to as a correctional center. This is in line with the current trend toward larger prison complexes, which share facilities.

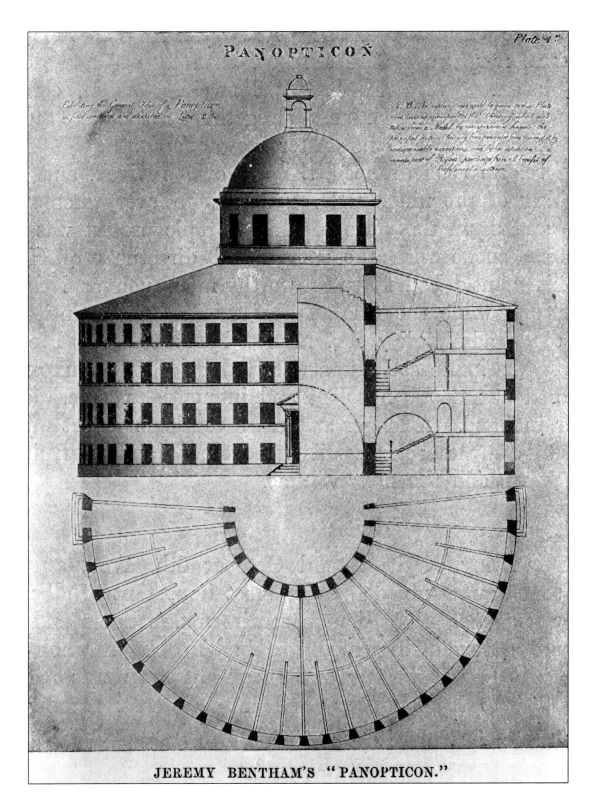

JEREMY BENTHAM'S "PANOPTICON."

This is Bentham's original panopticon drawing of 1791. Several panopticon prisons were built in Europe and the United States. One of the first, Western State Penitentiary in Pittsburgh, 1826, was a failure and was soon demolished.

Prisoners lined up in front of their cells in one of the large blocks at Stateville Penitentiary after the degrading lockstep was abolished. However, orderly lines were still maintained and strict discipline imposed by the prison officers.

BUT THEY WILL STILL TRY TO ESCAPE

To cope with the increase in crime, the Federal Bureau of Prisons and some states are clustering prisons. For example, one complex may house a facility with minimum-, medium-, and maximum-security capabilities fanning off central services, such as power plants, personnel offices, and security

TECHNOLOGY TO THE RESCUE

With correctional organizations bringing in more and more new technology, it is becoming more difficult to escape. Motion detectors attached to barbed wire and improved video surveillance help reveal and track unusual movements. The observation of prisoners in low light can be aided by thermal-imaging eyewear. Identification becomes easier by taking images of retinas, scanning hands, and using devices to analyze voices, while the development of nonlethal weapons, such as stun guns, should help stop the thwarting of escapes from turning into carnage. To prevent helicopter escapes, many prisons have strung cables across the prison yards.

monitoring blocks. Development of these complexes can also cut transportation costs between the types of prison and, should a disturbance or other event, such as a fire, occur, immediate backup is available from one of the other prisons.

Stateville is a 10-minute drive north of Joliet, but, despite never being on each other's doorsteps, the two prisons have shared much history since the 1920s. Some of it is bizarre—as revealed by the front pages of the *Chicago Herald-News*. In 1927, William Evans (an escapee from a prison in Missouri) decided he would free his old friend, Harry Funk, who was locked up in Joliet. Funk usually loaded furniture onto cars each afternoon by the prison's east gate. To gain access, William Evans dressed as a priest. The plan was to spirit Funk away in a stolen car. As part of a backup strategy, he took along a bottle of nitroglycerine with which to blast a hole into the prison wall. Unfortunately for Evans, the warden had already been informed of both plans and had moved Funk out to Stateville. He welcomed the priest in—and kept him: Evans was also a bank robber wanted in Illinois.

In 1935, another Joliet prisoner, Henry Ferneckes, bleached a prison uniform white, obtained a pair of sunglasses, and grew a mustache, which he concealed under a band-aid. At the front gate, Ferneckes pretended to be confused and handed the guard a note on which was the name of a convict in Stateville. He was duly directed there by a helpful prison official and made good his escape.

PUNISHMENT VS. REHABILITATION

In 1939, four Stateville lifers named Joyce, Jazorak, Balcurilis, and Hong thought up a new approach to escaping. They decided to drug the tower guards so that they would not see what was happening in the yard. The convicts ground up some hyoscine pills that they had stolen from the prison hospital. Hong, who prepared the guards' food, then dropped the powder into their coffee. Four of the tower guards drank it and passed out. The fifth

The door of a solitary confinement cell at Joliet Penitentiary in 1936. Such isolation, once usual under the separate system, is dreaded by some prisoners, who, wanting some social contact, might even prefer the endemic overcrowding elsewhere.

In the distance, Stateville's Assistant Warden tells Richard Speck, killer of eight nurses, that the Supreme Court has abolished the death penalty. Speck died in prison 20 years later in 1991.

took a sip, did not like the taste, and put it aside. Consequently, he stayed alert enough to spot three prisoners creeping toward the prison wall carrying a homemade ladder.

During the 1940s, Stateville was the venue of two mass-escape attempts. The first, in 1942, was successful. With the aid of a garbage truck and a ladder, nine prisoners got away. On that occasion, no shots were fired from the tower in case hostages were hit. In a similar attempt, in 1944, 10 convicts attacked four guards, tied them up, and raced across the prison yard in a truck. This time, four tower guards opened fire, not realizing there was a hostage, guard Zoeth Skaggs. He was killed instantly. Four convicts were wounded and one of them died two days later.

STATEVILLE TODAY

In 1987, during the filming of *Weeds*, starring Nick Nolte, at Joliet and Stateville, an inmate escaped in a film truck. Scenes for Oliver Stone's movie, *Natural Born Killers*, were also shot at Joliet and Stateville in 1993. "One crew member recalled the tension of filming," Frank Main reports—and some inmates were given gifts to keep the peace.

Through the years, U.S. prison policies have waxed and waned in favor of the punitive, then the liberal and rehabilitative. Mostly, there has been a gradual improvement in prison conditions. However, during the 1990s, there was a backlash due to the public perception that prisons had gone too soft. Many people thought that prisoners ought to work harder, be allowed less leisure time and fewer facilities, and their lives made tougher and grimmer. Some correctional jurisdictions even began reintroducing chain gangs and striped uniforms.

The debate still rages as to whether being denied one's freedom is punishment enough and that no further punitive restrictions should be applied. Of course, security problems remain. It will be interesting to see how correctional facilities develop during the 21st century, and whether the authorities will learn from the mistakes of the past.

STATEVILLE'S DEATH ROW

Stateville used to be home to one of the three electric chairs in Illinois, which were used 98 times between 1928 and 1962. The first to die by electric chair, on December 15, 1928, were three men convicted of murdering a farmer. The body of one of the men, John Brown, was unclaimed and has

been moldering in his grave in Stateville cemetery ever since.

One of Stateville's most high-profile recent executions (by lethal injection) was that of John Wayne Gacy (pictured). When not dressing as a clown and entertaining children for charity, Gacy murdered 33 boys and young men whose ages ranged from 9 to 27. He buried most of them in the crawl space beneath his house. Gacy's offenses were primarily committed in the 1970s. He was convicted in 1978, but not executed until 1994.

Meanwhile, he painted clown pictures in his cell, sent them to his pen pals, and recorded telephone messages that people paid good money to listen to. "It was shameful," wrote *Herald-News* city editor, John Whiteside, "not that we let Gacy die, but that it took place in such a full media blitz and allowed him to take his secrets with him." Thus, many parents would never know whether their children had been his victims.

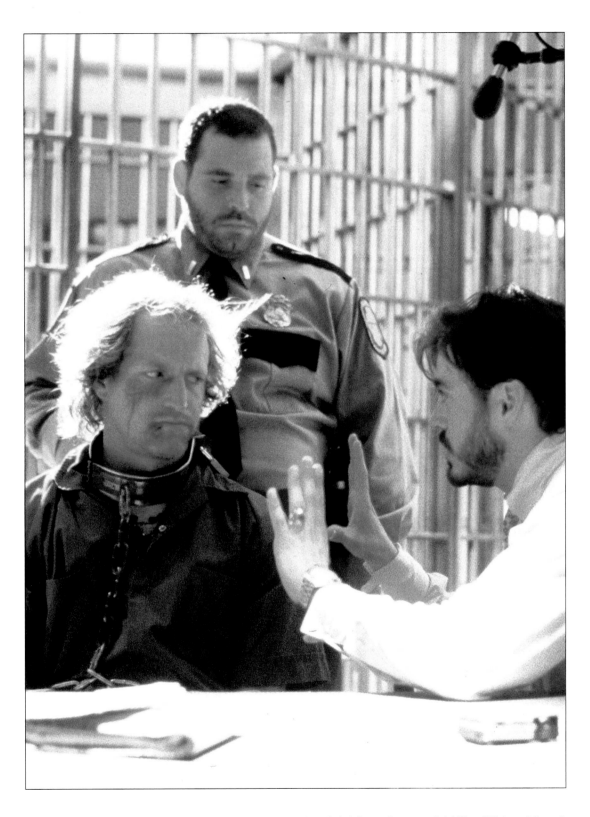

Here, cop Wayne Gayle (played by Robert Downey, Jr., right) interviews serial killer Mickey (played by Woody Harrelson, left), in Oliver Stone's blockbuster movie *Natural Born Killers*. Many scenes from the movie were shot at Stateville and Joliet penitentiaries.

GLOSSARY

Clemency: disposition to be merciful and especially to moderate the severity of punishment due

Fenians: association of Irish people founded in New York in 1857 for the overthrow of the British government in Ireland

Grievance: a real or imaginary wrong, for which there are thought to be reasonable grounds for complaint

Hulk: a ship used as a prison

Jute: the glossy fiber of either of two East Indian plants of the linden family, used chiefly for sacking, burlap, and twine

Lag: a convict

Launch (n.): a small motorboat that is open or that has the forepart of the hull covered

Lockstep: a mode of marching in step by a body of men, who move one after another as closely as possible

Obelisk: a square or rectangular pillar that tapers toward a pyramidal top

Orifice: any bodily opening

Panoptic: being or presenting a comprehensive or panoramic view

Parole: a conditional release of a prisoner serving an indeterminate or unexpired sentence

Perjury: giving false testimony while under oath

Phrenology: the study of the conformation of the skull based on the belief that it is indicative of mental faculties and character

Repatriation: returning a person to his or her country of origin

Rotunda: a building with a circular plan, and often with a dome

Screw (n.): slang term for a prison guard

Suffragettes: women who campaigned for all women to have the right to vote in elections

Throes: violent and involuntary muscle spasms, often caused by extreme pain

Vice: a moral fault or failing

Warder: a British prison guard, now known as a prison officer

Warden: head of a prison in the United States

CHRONOLOGY

1791:	Jeremy Bentham designs a panopticon prison.
1797:	Newgate Prison is built in Greenwich Village.
1809:	Dartmoor Prison is constructed; French prisoners arrive.
1812:	War between the United States and Britain.
1813:	American prisoners arrive at Dartmoor.
1814:	Napoleon is exiled to Elba; French prisoners are released.
1815:	Napoleon's return and Battle of Waterloo; French prisoners come back to Dartmoor; Napoleon exiled to St.Helena.
1815:	The Princetown Massacre.
1816:	Building begins on Auburn State Penitentiary; last French prisoners leave Dartmoor.
1825:	Building begins on Sing Sing.
1840:	Warden D.L. Seymour is appointed to Sing Sing.
1844:	Eliza Farnham becomes matron at Sing Sing.
1848:	California Gold Rush; Eliza Farnham resigns from Sing Sing.
1850:	Dartmoor is opened as a civil prison; Mountjoy Prison opens.
1852:	Devil's Island Prison opens.
1858:	Women's wing opened at Mountjoy; Joliet Penitentiary opens.
1865:	Mountjoy houses political prisoners.
1868:	Military prison is established on Alcatraz; Dartmoor memorial obelisks erected.
1871:	Tichborne Claimant civil case begins.
1874:	Tichborne Claimant goes to Dartmoor.
1877:	Closure of women's wing at Sing Sing.
1890:	Electric chair is introduced in the United States.
1891:	Sing Sing uses the electric chair for the first time.
1900:	Lockstep is abolished at Sing Sing.
1901:	Sing Sing is renamed Ossining.
1904:	Striped uniforms are abolished at Sing Sing.
1912:	Suffragettes are imprisoned in Mountjoy.
1914:	Rule of silence is abandoned at Sing Sing.
1916:	Easter Rising in Dublin.
1919:	Irish War of Independence.
1920:	Lewis E. Lawes is appointed warden at Sing Sing; 92 prisoners go on hunger strike in Mountjoy.
1921:	Signing of Anglo-Irish Treaty; Irish Civil War begins.
1922:	Seventy-seven republicans are shot in Irish prisons.

1923:   Irish Civil War ends.

1924:   First execution by gas chamber at San Quentin.

1928:   Ruth Snyder and Judd Gray are executed at Sing Sing; memorial gate to U.S. Dartmoor prisoners is erected; first escape by motorcar from Dartmoor; first execution by electric chair in Illinois.

1931:   Al Capone is arrested.

1932:   Mutiny at Dartmoor.

1933:   Justice Department purchases Alcatraz; Machine Gun Kelly kidnaps Charles Urschel.

1934:   Alcatraz opens as a federal penitentiary; silent and separate system is abandoned in Ireland.

1936:   Lucky Luciano is arrested; last execution by hanging at San Quentin.

1937:   Rule of silence is abolished at Alcatraz.

1938:   Escape attempt from Alcatraz.

1939:   Dock Barker's escape attempt from Alcatraz.

1940:   Warden Duffy is appointed to San Quentin.

1942:   Birdman arrives at Alcatraz; Brendan Behan goes to Mountjoy; mass escape from Stateville Penitentiary.

1944:   Mass-escape attempt from Stateville Penitentiary.

1946   Big Blast-Out at Alcatraz; Lucky Luciano is deported.

1948:   Brendan Behan is back in Mountjoy; Caryl Chessman is sentenced to death.

1953:   Julius and Ethel Rosenberg are executed at Sing Sing.

1954:   Brendan Behan is back in Mountjoy.

1960:   Caryl Chessman is executed at San Quentin.

1962:   George Jackson goes to San Quentin.

1963:   Alcatraz is deactivated; Sing Sing stops using the electric chair.

1966:   Frank Mitchell escapes from Dartmoor.

1970:   Soledad case.

1971:   George Jackson is killed at San Quentin.

1988:   Serial killer John Wayne Gacy is convicted.

1990:   Dartmoor Riot.

1991:   Damning report issued by the Mountjoy Visiting Committee.

1994:   John Wayne Gacy is executed at Stateville.

2000:   Proportion of the population of Irish women in Irish prisons is down to three percent.

FURTHER INFORMATION

Useful Web Sites

www.encyclopedia.com/html/D/Dartmoor.asp

www.execpc.com/~sril/dartmoor

www.geocities.com/MotorCity/Downs/3548/facility/singsing.html

www.hudsonriver.com/halfmoonpress/stories/0500sing.htm

www.notfrisco.com/calmen/sanquentin.html

www.turnpike.net/~mystery/tmg/san_Quentin.html

www.theweboftime.com/Issue-5/sanquentin.htm

Further Reading

Abbott, Jack Henry. *In the Belly of the Beast: Letters from Prison.* New York: Vintage Books, 1991.

Bunker, Edward. *Education of a Felon.* New York: Griffin, 2001.

Bunker, Edward. *Mr. Blue: Memoirs of a Renegade.* Harpenden, Hertfordshire: No Exit Press, 2000.

Carey, Tim. *Mountjoy: The Story of a Prison.* Cork: Wilton, 2000.

Conover, Ted. *Newjack: Guarding Sing Sing Today.* New York: Vintage Books, 2001.

Earley, Pete. *The Hot House: Life Inside Leavenworth Prison.* New York: Bantam Books, 1995.

Gordon, Robert Ellis. *The Funhouse Mirror: Reflections on a Prison.* Washington State University, 2000.

Publisher's note:
The Web sites listed on this page were active at the time of publication. The publisher is not responsible for Web sites that have changed their addresses or discontinued operation since the date of publication. The publisher will review and update the Web site list upon each reprint.

Hogshire, Jim. *You Are Going to Prison*. Yakima, WA: Breakout Productions, 1998.

Lerner, Jimmy. *You Got Nothing Coming: Notes from a Prison Fish*. New York: Broadway Books, 2002.

Robert, John Walter. *Reform and Retribution: An Illustrated History of American Prisons*. Lanham, Maryland: American Correctional Association, 1997.

Wynn, Jennifer. *Inside Riker's: Stories from the World's Largest Penal Colony*. New York: St. Martin's Press, 2001.

About the Author

A former officer with the Metropolitan Police in London, England, Joan Lock is an experienced writer specializing in police and criminal matters. Her non-fiction crime titles include *Lady Policeman, The British Policewoman, Marlborough Street: The Story of a London Court, Dreadful Deeds and Awful Murders, Scotland Yard Casebook,* and *Tales from Bow Street.*

Joan is also the author of four crime novels and was a regular contributor to *Police Review* magazine. She has also written dramatic plays and feature programs for BBC radio in England.

INDEX